LEARN TO RISE

Dr. Kavita Patni

TANEESHA PUBLISHING

ISBN : 9789347259289
Edition : First, December 2025
Title : Learn to Rise
Author : Dr. Kavita Patni

Published by

TANEESHA PUBLISHING

An Imprint of **Taneesha and Prachi NextGen Publication**

Registered Office: Sunil Complex, 2nd Floor, Vijay Nagar,
Western Kutchery Road, Meerut - 250002, Uttar Pradesh, India
Website : www.taneeshapublishing.com
E-mail : help@tpnextpub.com
Phone : 0121 453 0364

Printed by :
Manipal Technologies Limited, Bengaluru - 560001, Karnataka

INDEX

Preface

Life is a living process full of struggles, efforts and maintenance of one's inner being to get satisfied by working on one's own manner. Everybody has some wishes, some aims and some dreams to make true. For these to become part of life we need strong will and determination in our part. Keeping in mind the very demanding essentials of making a meaningful life the poetry collection- "Learn To Rise" has focused upon the real need and dealing which people have to understand to make a meaningful world. The Poems are written to give the message of love, care and harmony among people to bloom the flowers of real happiness and spread the fragrance of warmth in their surroundings. In today's world it is very necessary to keep the worth belongings of our cultures lively and proceed in an effective manner to make our stand with our traditional ethics.

In writing this poetry collection there is contribution of my well known relatives, friends, my kids and of course the school children with whom my most time is spent. Actually a person learns more by doing, therefore if we put honesty, dignity and courage in our work then certainly there is nothing that can't be achieved.

God give us strength to flourish,
To prosper the world is our wish.
The evils should never deter us,
Make us that strong and pious.

1. Where there is will there is a way

In the world of struggle today,
I want to remain in a soothing way.
Where there are no more wants,
I want to remain in a satisfied calm.

We thrive, we struggle the whole day long,
But with some failure and some success charms.
Our world moves in the direction of taste,
So let our will go into the success stage.

Where there is a will, there is always a way,
So let us make it desirable for success by pray.
Our world is made up of worries and rewards,
But it's up to you to deal and take success award.

Fill heart with courage and determination,
To go beyond skies of satisfaction.
Your will can move you go long in the race,
Almighty will give you all strength to face.

2. Work while work

There is a treasure in us,
If we work while we work.
You can achieve anything,
If you conquer your inner being.

When to start, on what to stay,
Makes the person's success all the way.
Dream hard, dream true,
Will make you successful too.

Do not end in just dreaming,
Be courageous to bring all well-being.
The soul you have got,
Is enough to deal any hard spot.

Be determined, be enthusiastic,
While working and you will be fantastic.
The dreams you see in the dark,
Desire your diligence in the day hours.

3. Sky is the limit

Either short or long life to exhibit,
Always know that sky is the limit.
To do a task is not hard,
But to keep determination in your part.

The world is miracle for those,
Who live with courage and purpose.
Those who strive for success in deeds,
Are truly appreciable and meet their needs.

The world Is like an open field,
Where you can sow happiness seeds.
Your efforts will move you forward,
So that you stand in any adverse.

The one who keeps will and courage,
Often leads the world with full grace.
We are self responsible for everything,
By determination you can get anything.

4. You can win

If you have will power within,
Then you can win.
Winning is not getting wealthy alone,
But to serve the world on your own.

To win is not only conquering others,
But to remain by good deeds in their hearts.
We will truly win in a good sense,
If it is working in society's upliftment.

The more you work, the more you learn,
And the wonderful keep on happen.
Trust in yourself and the almighty,
You will reach all the bounds with dignity.

Keep in mind the utter desire,
So that all world you an acquire.
To win in the true ways,
Can be hard but not so difficult always.

5. Life is a mystery

Life is puzzle, life is a mystery,
Be enthusiastic and live it fully.
It gives you many opportunities,
Grab them and get success with deeds.

Don't confuse on trifles,
Be determined to get good results.
If you initiate and hold the things,
You will be aspired to get everything.

Life is never a stoppage,
It's a struggle field from ages.
The history is witness of success,
Of those who lit their lamps in distress.

Life always leaves you with a hope or desire,
To do good for the society's honour.
A better soul always keeps in mind,
That we are born to make the world bind.

6. Heartfelt Thanks to God

The God is great to put life in us,
So that we prosper and meet purpose.
A heart felt thanks to the wealthy God,
Whose bag has no ends of offers.

Thanking God to make me see the world,
To understand the feeling of goodness and love.
Chirping birds and playing children on fields,
Are some soothing sights of His creativities.

The God is great all the time,
Making you comfortable in all regimes.
Whether easy or tough is the situation,
God gives you strength in all conditions.

Heart felt thanks to God to ignite my inner soul,
Whenever I need help and try my hard tools.
To make the situation calm and living,
Oh lovely God You are my everything.

7. Success depends on you

As we move ahead by virtues,
His graceful hands are always there too.
To acquire a lengthy wealth,
Is just a part but not the real strength.

Success comes all its way,
To the one who works hard with pray.
To initiate is the stepping stone,
By determination and courage results are shown.

We dream, we desire and we work,
But the correct direction make it all worth.
Try to do your best even in worst,
So that the flowers of success may burst.

Your will, your efforts can move you long,
There is no aim which you do not belong.
Make the light inside you always lightening,
To serve the earth in best ways of rewarding.

8. The dreams come true

When you are all through,
The dreams come true.
The dream of success and prosperity,
Often depends on your work with honesty.

When you dream big and high,
The work zeal always makes you drive.
The desire to meet your goals,
Is the ultimate lamp to get all.

The dreams big or small,
Come to success by efforts overall.
Always try to work hard,
So that you meet happiness yard.

The dreams of unity and integrity,
Will make the nation's prosperity.
Where there is no bar of rich and poor,
And every person remains in honour.

9. Every effort counts

In the world of struggle and humanity,
Everyone should work on one's dignity.
The problems the charms of belongings,
Should not affect you in your workings.

The one who initiates a work,
Should complete it with all efforts.
The efforts which are the results of determination,
Will propel you to reach the destination.

By keeping in mind the right and wrong,
Follow the path of justice and reach beyond.
The small efforts made by us,
Counts all and make everything worth.

The success stories are often written,
By those who are always good enough.
The hard work and dedicated efforts,
Always put milestones of successful years.

10. You are the Hero

In the world of struggle and pride,
You have to be enthusiastic and a hero beside.
The results which you grow,
Are often dependent on what you sow.

The world is full of opportunities,
It's up to you how to seize.
The ease and hardships are on the way,
To conquer difficulties is an art of life's way.

Dream big and do most for it,
May carry you ahead and let you uplift.
To dream is not enough to go,
But ultimately you have to be a hero.

There is nothing unattainable,
For the one who works hard and is capable.
The world of agony is far away,
For those who put efforts in their way.

11. The world is yours

Whether to love or to serve,
The world is always yours.
In the world of utter desire,
You can make your own empire.

To greet the things politely,
Will always make you smiling.
The thunders of difficulties,
Never touch the man with prompt deeds.

You can make the world good enough,
By making yourself rough and tough.
The world asks you your presence,
Therefore remain diligent and persistent.

God has given us a beautiful life,
Do goodwill and make everything delight.
Always keep do's and don'ts very fair,
So that there is no chance of shame anywhere.

12. Do what is right

In the whole journey of life,
Do always what is right.
The will can go here and there,
But you should be always fair.

The ups and downs of life,
Often makes you laugh or cry.
But to live a happy life,
Always remain consistent in tries.

The work of hardships always pay,
In one or another way.
Be determined and courageous,
You will always get deserving success.

By serving the world honestly,
You pave the path of great humanity.
By keeping wellness in surroundings,
Will help to become a good human being.

13. We the children of world

We the children of world,
Take oath to remain alert.
We are grateful to God for everything,
Who has provided us every belonging.

Right from the sunshine till sunset,
Give us tremendous energy and no rest.
We want to become big and high,
Give us strong wings to meet success skies.

And give trust and faith in us,
So that we don't harm anybody's heart.
Let us climb the success ladder,
To make our future secure and brighter.

The winds of sorrow will not deter us,
We will make the world shine by efforts.
Oh God give us strength and courage,
So that we make everybody praise.

14. Good deeds always count

In the world of nurturing and serving,
We do our best deeds in living.
To reach the success skies,
We should be good enough and wise.

The world is full of opportunities,
We have to work to accomplish these.
The God is always with us,
We will never break His trust.

Good deeds make everyone happy,
And also bring all prosperity.
The way you choose to deal,
Should be perfect to succeed in every zeal.

The world full of colours of joys,
Always welcome you with love enormous.
Good deeds will never make you fall,
They will always make you prosper and do well.

15. God give me strength

Oh God give me strength,
Give me courage to defend.
The worries of world will never break me,
With entire will and enthusiasm, I will be ready.

The dreams of success and happiness,
Will be fulfilled by working endless.
The efforts we put altogether,
Will always make us prosper and not deter.

Make me eligible to write fortune,
Of honour and high succession.
By Your blessings of love and care,
We will make the prosperity and be happier.

The trust You put in us for service,
Will never be shattered at any hardship.
We will make the world meaningful,
By becoming honest and truthful.

16. You can bring the happiness

In this world of love and hatred,
It's only you who can bring happiness.
The clouds of worries and difficulties,
Can be eradicated by wise efforts with ease.

The world we make today,
Will serve the ages all way.
The world of struggle and humanity,
Is dependent on our good deeds.

Always do what is right in manner,
To serve goodness in the world ever.
The learnings of hardships and courage,
Will pave the path of honour at all stages.

The dreams of success and prosperity,
Will come true by working continuously.
The great God has blessed us with strength,
So we have to meet success at every end.

17. Living a meaningful life

Living a meaningful life,
Fill us with love and pride.
The people who do remarkable jobs,
Are always praised in all.

Always do the meaningful works,
Rather than spending time on talks.
Your efforts will raise you ahead,
And will make the life beautiful and best.

Make your ways bright and beautiful,
For mankind's harmony and be fruitful.
The sky is the limit for those,
Who are always on the way of endeavour.

The world remains good and adorable,
For those who are always diligent and eligible.
The God has provided us every blessing,
Build your life strong and winning.

18. The lovely life

Thank you God for giving me life,
I will make it always a pride.
The sun in the noon and moon in the night,
Lead me the way of justice and right.

The chirping birds in the sky,
Fill the world of happiness in life.
The shooting mountains on the earth,
Teach us the lesson not to deter.

The people of the world big or small,
Are the signs of divine power in them all.
The world surrounded by the rivers and oceans,
Saying that the water in them is also precious.

The stars and planets in the universe,
Make us learn the happenings clusters.
Be he, be she, be you or be I,
Are all enjoying this beautiful life.

19. Be living Always

The God has showered the blessings in life,
They are mean to accomplish good works all wise.
Be living not just by presence,
But like the flowers spreading fragrance.

The life of those succeeds,
Who are always on the way to proceed.
Life means to move ahead,
Not to waste time on regrets.

The life is a living river,
Which has to meet the sea of victories.
Move ahead and do not set back,
The ongoing time calls your effort attack.

Make your will good and strong,
So that you reach success beyond.
The desire of getting prosperity,
Is achieved by a truly living heart indeed.

20. Work is worship

In the world of hardships,
To remember is work is worship.
The God remains in every work and in us,
Therefore do efforts with good hearts.

Work honestly while you work,
With a vision to serve the world.
Your works, your deeds,
Should prosper the humanity indeed.

The works of goodwill and honesty,
Pays to the world with all prosperity.
Ignore all the nonsense that seize you,
Have strong hearts to reach success sky too.

Your work is always a worship for you,
And the God certainly helps you.
The true devotee of the God,
Offers good servings in the world of lord.

21. Serve the mankind

God has provided us skills of different kinds,
So that we prosper and serve best to the mankind.
Every effort of yours should be genuine,
And you hit the target of life benign.

Will to make world wonderful,
Will make you prosper and successful.
The strength of goodness and care,
Always make the world of fair.

Try to do good works around,
So that you reach destiny bounds.
In the meaningful life of God,
We shall make the prosperity way long.

The God has given enough power in us,
To do well and serve better.
The dreams of unity and integrity,
Will be fulfilled by keeping efforts consistently.

22. My Country

My country long and wide,
Is my birth place with all delight.
My childhood as I remember,
Was fulfilled with love and laughter.

The country's wellness and pride,
Depends on our deeds of wise.
The country people and country's wealth,
All prosper with good minds and health.

My country where the pious rivers flow,
Igniting our minds to and fro.
The standing mountains on this crust,
Save us from wind blows and enemy's thrust.

My country, my faith, my love,
Will remain always horizon above.
Every success is yours dear country,
Which we will achieve and make it a history.

23. You deserve the best

Be it's life upliftment or rest,
Always remember you deserve the best.
By making soul true and loving,
We can achieve anything.

The deeds of success are done,
By working continuously in persistence.
The good works are often counted,
In the chapters of history content.

The good works make you rise and shine,
Like a moon among the stars in the skies.
The goodness is a great virtue,
For which we should always be due.

Our wealth, our fortune, all is fine,
But be humane is most important refine.
The earth beneath and the sky above,
Wants the goodwill of successful world.

24. The successful life

Dreaming low or dreaming high,
Different aspects of successful life.
A person's life is only successful,
If he is living it lively and be fruitful.

One's own success is different,
But to serve successfully is important.
The world of honour and pride,
Is truly dependent on one's goodwill side.

The successful life fills your heart,
With responsibilities and not only with lustres.
A successful man always make destiny,
Of good culture and humanity.

A successful man leads the life,
Rather than those who only survive.
To make the world all prosperous,
It is necessary that we all be adventurous.

25. You can reach the success horizon

By working hard and with determination,
You can reach the success horizon.
The dreams of happiness and prosperity,
Are met by those who are always steady.

Success fruits will be to you early or delay,
Depending on your efforts and working way.
It is not difficult to get good results,
But only in the difference of struggle manners.

Work with a vision and focus,
Will always lead you to the success.
The works in one while or other,
Often leads to the failure.

To succeed alone is not sufficient,
To have success in the surroundings is important.
The world is full of success colours,
You can achieve them in one way or other.

26. Life is to honour

Life gives us many things,
We are bestowed by its every blessing.
Life is to live happily and fully,
And spread the fragrance of goodness utterly.

Life is to give honour to all,
Who have helped you in the life's protocol.
The more you learn, the more you offer,
Makes the surroundings happy and prosper.

The almighty God has created us,
To be enthusiastic and courageous.
We should not be sad or coward,
Rather face the problems with full efforts.

To give honour and respect others,
Is the quality of life's great leaders.
The love and care you offer,
Always return to you in good manner.

27. The wish to succeed

The wish to succeed, the wish to prosper,
Comes true by putting strong efforts.
The wish to become a doctor,
Should help the society to be healthier.

The wish to become an engineer,
Should build strong buildings and all repair.
If you wish to be an astronaut,
The universe should be in your knot.

The wish to become a teacher,
Should spread the knowledge in all spheres.
If you wish to be an artist,
Dancing and singing should be fit.

If you wish to be an actor,
Should show the learned things in the world.
The wish that encompasses all the horizons,
Is the wish and will to become a good citizen.

28. Life is a struggle

Life is a struggle full of stories,
Of warm wishes and success victories.
Every struggle is for living,
Either to survive or winning.

Struggle like sun in the sky,
To shine for warmth and light.
Struggle like moon in night dark,
Which shows the path and sparks.

Struggle like mountains and rivers,
To stand still and flow for ever.
Struggle like the wind that blows,
To spread prosperity in all spheres.

Struggle for the world like great persons do,
To uplift society's honour and respect too.
To struggle can vary person to person,
But to keep efforts in right direction.

29. Make yourself Happy

To live lively and effectively,
All you need is to be happy.
The work you are doing happily,
Has different impact on the society.

If your heart is filled with humour,
You can get heights of honour.
The people with sad minds and hearts,
Require healthy habits of living and conduct.

A happy soul always care for others,
By good efforts and healthy culture.
It is necessary to keep your heart happy,
To be in right direction for prosperity.

The divine soul in us,
Is made to make world prosperous.
Being be happy we make healthy surroundings,
And this is the need of hour's for well being.

30. The Goodwill Always Works

A goodwill always works,
Whether while working or in actions.
A goodwill opens your way,
Of prosperity and happiness passages.

A goodwill helps you to improve,
Your own character and society's status too.
A goodwill is always true and kind,
To make the world beautiful and all refined.

The people with goodwill,
Are sufficient to eradicate every evil.
The goodwill binds you with enthusiasm,
To work honestly and do others no harm.

The goodwill always pave your path,
With success and good rewards.
The goodwill of all of us,
Make the world shining in all spheres.

31. Make me a great soldier

To serve my country in the world,
Make me a soldier dear Lord.
I will fight with the enemies,
And will bring victory and peace.

Oh God fill my heart with true patriotism,
So that country is safe in all timings.
Fill me with immense power and strength,
That the enemy finds no way to stand.

My country, my pride, my honour,
Will never fall by anyone who dishonour.
My country is my heart my soul,
I will prosper it by saving it and servng too.

The country where I born and brought up,
Will always remain all above.
My country which is great and my pride,
In difficulties becomes like a bride.

32. My beautiful Home

My beautiful home, my heart, my love,
In the whole world it is all above.
My parents who let me learn the ethics,
Will never make me fall in difficulty.

My home a place of God's worshipping,
Where the bells ring at night and in the morning.
My home full of love and laughter,
Where together with care live brothers and sisters.

The home where I get divine parental education,
Which is best and full of dedication.
The wishes and cheers all are fulfilled,
Like a dream land which offers everything.

My beautiful home should always prosper,
This is my desire from bottom of my heart.
The manners and servings inculcated in me,
Can make me to reach any destiny.

33. Make your life healthy

Early to bed early to rise,
Are good habits to remain best and nice.
A healthy body has a healthy mind,
Remember this thought all the time.

A healthy soul thinks better,
And has great servings to offer.
Eat healthy, do not overload,
A balanced diet will always be good.

A healthy state of mind is fantastic,
To do progress and get every target.
Eating healthy foods and no junks,
Will make strong body and heart.

A healthy life is a boon for society,
To maintain the surroundings clean with dignity.
The healthy habits of good culture,
Make you rise in the struggling world.

34. Go green go green

In the world of living beings,
It is necessary today to go green and green.
The cutting of trees in the forest,
Is sign of fall and life unrest.

The green trees provide fresh air and good vision,
Which is necessary for life's extension.
The falling forests today for buildings and market,
Bring to us draught and make environment upset.

Go green, go green is the need of hour,
So that we and Earth stand in power.
The greenery around soothes heart and minds,
And fills the surroundings with clean air besides.

The three R's are very useful,
Reduce, Reuse and Recycle.
Planting trees in abundance,
Can save the earth from pollution and decadence.

35. Inculcate Good Habits

Inculcate good habits of living,
To make a healthy life and keep going.
Good habits boost your heart with culture,
Of good living and manner.

To learn good and do wise,
Are the habits of making everybody surprise.
The good you learn the good you serve,
To make the humanity prosperous.

Working with a healthy and good mind,
Will not remain any mistake behind.
The good habits of love and care,
Will never led you alone and despair.

The world of God is made,
To live together and to stop hatred.
The God will also be happy to see His creativity,
In a prosperous and successful dignity.

36. Make the Surroundings clean

Make the surroundings green and clean,
By making it a habit from within.
The clean surroundings often develop,
Good society with cultured manner and conduct.

The clean surroundings make you feel,
That cleanliness is necessary for healthy zeal.
Do not litter or spit here and there,
This everybody has to take care.

The clean surroundings make you happy,
To make the world shine and ready.
The clean you remain inside out,
Helps in making you all proud.

The world is beautiful when clean,
To make everybody rise and win.
The clean surroundings make your mind healthy,
To live successfully and happily.

37. Be Good and Good be to you

Be good and wise to others,
That will reflect to you in different manner.
The good going in behaviour,
Will give you a lot of pleasure.

The good you do in works,
Always pays you best in perks.
The goodness of a man always remains in heart,
Like an encouraging tool of achievement.

This is the nature's rule divine,
That you will get what you are sowing.
The nature of love and care,
Often brings happiness and favour.

The good you do for the society,
Also helps yourself and everybody.
There should not be discrimination in offerings,
Because you will get the same receiving.

38. The School Days

Everyone of us once a time,
Meet the school regime.
The time we move to school,
We are bound by discipline and rules.

The school building the school ground,
Are all marvellous to spread knowledge bounds.
The school days with lovely prays and chants,
Fulfill us with great energy and success.

In the school we learn how to grow,
That too in the right direction of flow.
We come to learn the do's and don'ts,
That are very helpful to go beyond.

To become a doctor or an engineer,
Whether to be an artist or a teacher.
It is very necessary to remember,
The precious lessons of school chamber.

39. The festivals of India

India the land of colours and beauty,
Hold different cultures in it's vicinity.
The country is honoured with love and humour,
To remain successful be prosper.

The colours of Holi and sparks in Deepawali,
All bring the lesson of unity in diversity.
The blooming flowers in Basant Panchami,
Send the message of growth and fertility.

The Bhangra, the Onam and Rakshabandhan,
All fulfill the hearts with delight and satisfaction.
The Eid moon and the ringing bells of Christmas,
Bring immense prosperity and happiness cultures.

Oh God We live together and happily,
With no means to harm the humanity.
Give us will and courage enough,
That we don't fight ever over trifles.

40. My dream is my dream

Right from the opening eyes in mother's lap,
A world of wishes and desires is met.
To jump out and see the world is the first wish,
Then to meet our goal is the ever going wish.

Dream big or dream small,
My dream is my dream all above.
Whether to climb a mountain top,
Or to remain in the struggle of becoming boss.

My dreams to come true,
Truly require my efforts to put through.
The dreams turn into reality,
When we put works and mind in them utterly.

The dreams move the whole life long,
Make them marvellous and prompt.
The way we think the way we move,
Make the dreams all alive and true.

41. Let me where there is no limit

Oh God above in the heaven,
Listen to my this prayer on the earth garden.
Give me strength and courage indeed,
To reach the success all limits.

Make my way Where there is no limit,
To spread love and affection with all hits.
To mould hatred into care and wisdom,
Let me drive to that level of kingdom.

The world is full of sorrows and worries,
Make me capable to handle all these.
Give me power to surpass all challenges,
And fill my heart with love and kindness.

Make me so strong make me so powerful,
That the evil deeds remain far away from my soul.
Bless me with strength to serve humanity,
And my works always find place in dignity.

42. The world is beautiful

See inside or see outside,
The God has created us very right.
The chirping birds the blue skies,
Are all creations of God's might.

The world is beautiful or can be made,
By worthy deeds and good vision intake.
The world full of lovely opportunities and aims,
Focus us to chase them with all strengths.

The sun rays and the moon light,
Make our living easy in the day and night.
The world full of beautiful people around,
Who spread their culture and religious sounds.

Take it as an opportunity to serve in the world,
With wise means and kind words.
Beware of doing any harm to others,
As the world is flourished by making offer.

43. The Beauty of Mind

The beauty of mind lies in nurturing,
The world around us with all willing.
The more you offer the more you prosper,
This is the ultimate nature's culture.

The beautiful mind is expressed there,
Where there is healing for others care.
The beauty of mind lies not only on oneself,
But to promote the humanity's progress.

Let us shine and let us rise,
To make the world a beautiful paradise.
You don't know when and where,
Your good works will pay you offer.

Do good enough for the world,
And make your life a great build up.
The ups and downs are on their parts,
But should not deter you in doing good efforts.

44. My story of life

My story of splendid life,
A bit dark and lot of light.
The story covers the glimpses of childhood,
Followed by the struggle for success by youth.

The story is full of love and laughter,
With the people before and thereafter.
The making of life for different purposes,
Often excel me to meet the successes.

Always remember In your mind,
For a successful life there are struggles behind.
The success is to maintain flow of love and care,
So that our birth on this earth Is fair.

The story of life is still continued,
And the Almighty give me strength to do good.
Oh God prosper me to face all conditions,
And I come up with all the solutions.

45. Our will decides our ways

To overcome the difficulties in our life,
It is judicious to take clever decisions and be wise.
The will to proceed for better and success,
Should always be enlightened to progress.

Our will is the way to proceed ahead,
To reach the destination with ill thoughts neglect.
We make our world of prosperity and glory,
By being determined and working till eternity.

The world is great and divine,
We can accomplish our works by being fine.
Our inner strength can push us forward,
In every circumstances and work demand.

The dreams we see in the night,
Are made true with all our power inside.
To become good enough is not complete,
But to drive the society is the need.

46. The world of prosperity

In the world of many possibilities,
Everyone desires the success with prosperity.
The success is the part of life,
But a good vision should be the drive.

Making one's world by cheating and fooling,
Remains no more but only ruining.
The God has blessed us with all wills,
To choose the right ones is our skill.

Our world of struggle and efforts,
Should make a good world to nurture.
We should do something justified always,
So that a good society is always paved.

The world of honour and pride,
Depends on our deeds of good sacrifice.
The prosperity remains throughout the life,
If we work for humanity's progress and thrive.

47. Let us unite

Let us unite to make country proud,
To reach every successful bound.
Let us unite to bring the glory,
By defeating the enemies on the boundary.

Being united we can make innings,
That are all wonderful and winning.
A single stick can be broken at once,
But the bundle is not broken by anyone.

By the power of unity and integrity,
Our nation can meet the success destiny.
Stay united to face the evil,
Stay united to kill the devil.

United community has a great effect,
To tackle the evil situation at its best.
United we stand divided we fall,
This is the ultimate need and time call.

48. The Desire of becoming a good human

Oh God either make me a doctor or a teacher,
To heal patient and impart knowledge to poor.
By becoming a scientist or engineer,
I should explore space and become creator.

By becoming a chef or a plumber,
I should serve good food and fix all the repairs.
The desire of becoming an astronaut or mason,
Will explore space and do maintenance.

The wish to become a pilot or a sea diver,
For safe landings and recreations underwater.
If I could be a leader or an actor,
The aim is of a good nation and humour.

The desires are endless and wishes are high,
But God make me one feel pride.
By the works of goodwill and honesty,
My life should shine by honouring humanity.

49. The Beauty of Flowers

The beautiful flowers in the world,
Are signs of dignity and good efforts.
They bring the sensation of good look,
And make us happy with the smell good.

The beautiful flowers for God's worship,
Are used to address our feelings.
Flowers in the functions flowers in the party,
Make all happy and feel positivity.

The beautiful flowers with or without thorn,
Have importance and teach us to be prompt.
Like flowers we all should grow,
To maintain the world beautiful and glow.

Like the flowers we spread fragrance of truth,
By being honest and wisdom full.
Like the flowers we maintain beauty,
Of great honour and dignity.